Given To ~~_____~~

From ~~_____~~

Date *August 3, 1971*

A gift of appreciation for someone special.

ABOUT THE AUTHOR

Donald E Wildmon is minister of Lee Acres United Methodist Church in Tupelo, Mississippi. His weekly inspirational column entitled "Whatsoever Things" is carried in several newspapers and magazines across the country. He is the author of several other books listed by title on page 5.

Mr. Wildmon is a graduate of Millsaps College and Emory University. A person who loves to travel, he annually leads a tour of the Holy Land. Christians from across the country join Mr. Wildmon on his tours and he gives an invitation to anyone who would be interested in accompanying him on a tour to contact him through the publishers.

Stepping Stones

By Donald E. Wildmon

★ ★ ★ ★ ★

Five Star Publishers
Box 1368
Tupelo, Mississippi 38801

For
My Brothers—
JOHNNY *and* ALLEN

Other Books By Donald E. Wildmon

NUGGETS OF GOLD
THOUGHTS WORTH THINKING
A GIFT FOR LIVING
PEBBLES IN THE SAND
TREASURED THOUGHTS

Ask for them at your favorite store.

★ ★ ★ ★ ★
FIVE STAR PUBLISHERS
BOX 1368
TUPELO, MISSISSIPPI 38801

"Good Reading Comes From Five Star"

The Stones

A Stone On:
"I DIDN'T THINK YOU WOULD"

Malachi 3:8—*"Will man rob God? Yet you are robbing me. But you say, 'How are we robbing thee?' In your tithes and offerings."*

Somewhere I came across a story which kinda took me by surprise. It's the story of a man who was being checked by the Internal Revenue Department concerning his income tax return. And in that respect he had something in common with many of us. For occasionally our Uncle Sam wants to see the proof that we did what we said we did with our money.

It seems as though this particular gentleman was being asked to produce records which substantiated some of his claims made when he filed his income tax return. The fellow who was doing the questioning was rather short and rude with the man, and was actually treating the man as though he had told a lie about every deduction made on his return.

When questioned about his travel expenses, the gentleman produced records which showed that he had spent exactly what he had said he spent. Then the Internal Revenue agent asked him to produce records concerning his medical expenses. The gentleman reached into his file, pulled out his medical expense statements, and laid them on the table before the agent. Upon close examination the agent found that the man had had extremely high medical expenses that year due to the illness of his wife. But the records were in order and it was evident that he had spent exactly what he had said he had spent on medical expenses.

Going on down the line of deductions, the agent came upon the gentleman's gifts to his church. "All right," said the agent, "let's see your records on what you say you gave to the church." The comment was made in a rather derogatory manner and carried with it a suggestion that it was at this point that the gentleman had lied about his tax deductions. The fellow again reached down into his file, pulled out his cancelled checks made out to his church, and laid those on the table.

One by one, adding them as he went, the agent examined the checks. Upon adding the total amount, the agent found that the gentleman had given to the penny that which he had said he had given. Half apologizing and half angry because he had not found an error, the agent explained: "I had to check your records. I didn't believe you had given that much to your church. That's more than ten percent of your total income. Lots of folks say they give a lot to the church but when an examination is made it's a whole lot less. I just didn't believe you had given that much to your church," the agent concluded. "I didn't think you would," was the gentleman's only reply. The agent didn't know exactly what he meant by it, but let it slide.

The following Sunday, that tax agent felt a need to attend church. He didn't attend much but felt, since he was in a trying period of problems, that he would give it a try. As the offering plate passed, he dropped in a dollar bill. As he did, he saw a check in the plate written by the man he had questioned just that week. Looking up, he saw the gentleman sitting in the pew in front of him. Looking back down at the offering plate again, he saw his dollar beside the man's check. Suddenly the full impact of the gentleman's closing statement dawned on him. "I didn't think you would."

We have a terrible tendency to judge others by our own stinginess.

A Stone On:
THE FELLOW WHO FORGOT HIS SERMON

Matthew 12:34b—*"For out of the abundance of the heart the mouth speaks."*

The little village church was crowded. The congregation was waiting anxiously to hear the message that the speaker was to bring. It was no ordinary occasion. For a hometown boy was about to preach his first sermon.

As the young Methodist preacher arose to speak, he gave evidence of doing some extensive homework for his sermon. The fact that he was a very educated person was one which he wished for the people to immediately recognize. For three weeks the young man had worked on that sermon, making sure that it was a sermon of the highest intellectual stature.

He was doing pretty good with his sermon, impressing the people with his brilliant mind, when he happened to use a very intellectual word to impress the people. One young lady, sitting on the front row, evidently not able to comprehend some of the preaching from such an intelligent person, snickered when the young preacher used the word.

In fact, she hid her face to keep from laughing out loud.

It was a very disturbing experience for the young preacher. The snickering upset him so much that he forgot the rest of his sermon. Very badly embarrassed at the situation, the young man soon admitted to the congregation that he had forgotten the rest of his sermon. As he headed toward his seat, a thought ran through his mind. "Well, you can't remember your sermon. But isn't there anything that Christ has done for you that you can tell them?"

Immediately the young preacher turned and headed back to the pulpit. And so, for the second time that day, he proceeded to tell, in a spirit of enthusiasm, of what the Carpenter of Men had done for him.

After the service was over another young man came up to the preacher and said he wanted Christ to do the same thing for him that He had done for the young preacher. And so the first of countless opportunities to spread the Good News was opened to the young preacher who had forgotten his sermon.

I think there is a lesson for us here. Our Creator doesn't need someone down here on earth to use their brilliant and intellectual minds to impress folks. What He wants and needs is someone with heart enough to simply tell what He has done for us. For the greatest preaching isn't to be done through the brain—as important as that part of the body is to every minister. The greatest preaching with the most far-reaching effects comes from the heart—from one who can say, "This I know God can do, for He has done it for me."

Being a minister, I believe I need all the education and study I can get. And I have spent the greater part of my life pursuing it—and still do. But I have found that what does the most good is not an intellectual sermon, but a simple sermon from the heart which folks know to be true.

Perhaps the best thing that ever happened to E. Stanley Jones was that he forgot his first sermon and spoke from the heart. And maybe it will happen again—to each of us.

A Stone On:
THE WONDER OF WORDS

Proverbs 15:23b—*"And a word in season, how good it is!"*

Did you ever notice the wonder of words? They have the power to heal or to hurt, to stab or to soothe, to lift or to level. And in that respect, each of us were created equal. That is, we can use or abuse this wonderful power of the spoken word.

It is easy to be cutting in one's remarks. And certainly this is the tempting route sometimes. All of us have, at some time in our life, experienced the very deep hurt that comes from the cutting remarks. And, beyond a doubt, each of us has been guilty of expressing cutting remarks ourself.

For words to cut deeply into one's heart doesn't mean they have to be spoken with malice or prejudice. Indeed, the deepest hurt comes from words spoken apart from malice or prejudice. For those who speak with malice or prejudice usually have very little, if any, concern for those they speak against. But let one who is supposed to love us speak a selfish word to us and the cut goes into the quick.

Two young men were called upon one day to

13

give a dramatic reading before a very select audience. One of the young men was a very intelligent, very seasoned performer. He had the ability to hold the audience in his grip. The other young man was not so seasoned, had not the opportunity for experience. But he had one quality which was a part of him more than anything else—he wanted to become an actor. More than anything in all the world, he wished to be an actor.

The first young man went before the crowd polished and perfect—except for one slight flaw in pronouncing a word. When he walked off the stage his mother was waiting for him. She immediately began condemning the young man because he made the single mistake. She said nothing about the rest of the speech which was absolutely perfect. The only thing the young man could hear from the lips of his mother was condemnation for only a slight error—a slip of the tongue. The mother acted as if she was embarrassed by the son's mistake.

The second young man went on the stage. He mispronounced several words, forgot his script in three places, and in general gave a very poor amateur performance. But the audience could tell that the young man was trying, trying as hard as he could. When he walked from the stage he was utterly disgusted with his performance and vowed to do better next time. But his mother, waiting for him as he stepped from the stage, put her arms around him and said to him in a voice of love:

"I'm proud of you, son. You did the best you could. You will do better next time."

Yes, it is rather strange the power that words have. It costs nothing more to speak constructively than it does cuttingly. It takes no more breath to speak helpful words than it does hurting words. And the constructive and helpful words do so much more good.

If you were coming down from the stage, which words would you like to hear? The rest of us would, also. Let's try to speak them.

A Stone On:
WHEN ONE DOOR CLOSES, ANOTHER OPENS

Mark 10:27b—*"For all things are possible with God."*

He was a little man. Stood just a little over five feet tall. Weighed not much more than a young boy. But when he rose to speak, crowds numbering in the thousands would listen in awe to him. Thousands upon thousands responded to his plea.

As a child he barely escaped death from burning. Some enemies of his father set fire to his home. As the family escaped, they thought all the children were safe. His mother looked back at the burning house and saw his face filled with fear pressed against a window. Some neighbors went to his rescue and pulled him from the burning house.

Even though he had eighteen brothers and sisters, only four younger than he, there was still enough love to go around for him. His mother constantly saw to it that she spent some time alone with him, as well as each of her other children. His father was a preacher, and the family had a hard time just managing to get by.

As an adult he entered the ministry, and served well in the service of the Creator. He came to America to preach before the United States of America came into being. Failing in his preaching ministry in America, as well as being rejected in a love affair, he packed his bags and headed home for England a dejected man.

Soon after he had returned to England, he had an experience with the Carpenter of Galilee which was not only to drastically change his life but alter the lives of millions of other people around the world. He became so fervent with his preaching that one of the churches where he preached informed him that he was not to preach in that church again. The church was like most of the churches in England at that time—cold, formal, ritualistic. It wasn't long before he received notices from other churches in England that he was not to preach in them again, either. And in time he found that all the churches were closed to him, and the Church of England—of which he was a member—no longer had a place for him.

He was invited to preach in the open countryside to the common folk, but declined. He thought it beneath his dignity and the dignity of the Good News he preached to preach in the open air. One day, however, he swallowed his pride and went into the open air to preach. It was the beginning of a way of preaching which he would follow for the rest of his life.

Not only did this man influence the religious

life of England, but he also fought for and helped secure better social conditions for the poorer people. His followers wanted him to withdraw from the Church of England and begin a new movement, but he never consented to it. He died refusing to part with the Church of England.

John Wesley fell in love with the Galilean Fisher-of-Men at Aldersgate. This meant he fell in love with the people, also. Finding the doors closed to him in the place where he wanted to proclaim the Good News, he turned in another direction where his Creator had opened the door.

It is an example we could still follow. For you see, when one door closes, another opens.

A Stone On:
GIVING WHAT YOU HAVE GOT

Mark 8:34b—*"If any man would come after me, let him deny himself and take up his cross and follow me."*

One day in London a Methodist preacher looked out on the poor people of that city. His heart went out to those people. He wanted to help them. And he dedicated his life to their service. Little did he know what that dedication would mean.

In a few years his efforts to aid the poor had gained a few followers, and many opponents. Quite often he found his followers beaten and their property wrecked or destroyed because of their convictions. In 1884, 37 years after he began preaching, six hundred of his followers were sent to prison because of their religious concern for the poor.

Following several years of persecution, the founder and the movement began to win some acceptance. Much of this acceptance was brought about when he presented his case in a book entitled "In Darkest England And The Way Out." In that book he had concrete proposals for several improvements: relieving pauperism and fighting vice; homes for the homeless; training centers to prepare emigrants for overseas countries; rescue homes for women and girls being sold into bondage for immoral purposes; homes for released prisoners; legal aid for the poor; and practical help for the alcoholic.

The movement became known as the Salvation Army, and the preacher who fell in love with the poor people of London was named William Booth. Someone asked him one day what the secret of his very productive life was. His answer was simple, and quite profound: "I will tell you the secret," he said. "I have made up my mind that Jesus Christ could have all there was of William Booth. I know that He has men with more brains and more ability. But when I saw the poor of London, and, knowing what Jesus Christ could do for them, I made up my mind to give all there is of me to Him." Of this man, the historian wrote that his theology was "simple, certainly concentrated on essential matters, clearly expounded for the understanding and inspiration of the common man."

Read the history books and one thing stands out above everything else—it isn't the man with the most ability who does the most good in life. It is, rather, the man with the most dedication and determination. And herein is the beauty of the Christian faith. For the Carpenter doesn't judge us by how much ability we have, but by the depth of our dedication. It isn't the wisest man, or the richest man, or the strongest man that the Galilean is looking for. No! It is the dedicated and faithful man.

Our Maker doesn't judge us by how high we rise in life, but by how hard we try. We aren't judged by the amount of our abilities, but by the way we use what abilities we have. William Booth made up his mind to give all he had. That's all our Maker wants.

I guess what this story really says to us is that when we present ourselves to Him for service, we should leave our credentials and recommendations at home. We need to bring only our faithfulness.

A Stone On:
THE CHURCH WILL PREVAIL

Matthew 16:18—*"And I tell you, you are Peter, and on this rock I will build my church, and the powers of death shall not prevail against it."*

After he lost a bid for re-election, City Councilman Walter E. Berrick, Jr., of Danville, Virginia, filed a campaign expense account of $79.81. The final entry was 62¢ for aspirin!

And every mother knows which side the bread is buttered on—the side the kids drop on the kitchen floor!

Because his vehicle was getting low on gas, R.J. Burns stopped at a service station in Kannapolis, North Carolina, and said, "Please fill 'er up." Admittedly, there's nothing unusual about that except that Burns was at the controls of a helicopter and not a car!

An editor received a story from one of his reporters about the theft of 2,025 pigs from one farmer, said the Van Horn, Texas, weekly *Advocate*. Curious about the large number, he called the farmer. "Are you the one who had 2,025 pigs stolen?" the editor asked. "Yeth, I thure am," replied the farmer. "Thanks," said the editor. He rewrote the story to report the theft of two sows and 25 pigs. Oh, me! You can't win them all! It was a thad thory.

Then there is the true story of what happened up in Ohio. The residents of Bazetta Township are waging war against a chicken farmer whose stock they say is odiferous. They are taking the case to court. But until the court decides something, they have satisfied themselves with this sign by the town limits: "Entering Stinkville, population 72,000 stinking chickens. Unfit for human habitation."

Out in Longview, Texas, the policeman read the note on the windshield of a car parked in a no parking area. It read: "I have circled this block 10 times, and I have an appointment and must keep it or lose my job. Forgive us our trespasses." The officer wrote a note of his own and left it on the windshield. It read: "I have circled this block for 20 years. If I don't give you a ticket I will lose my job. Lead us not into temptation."

Finally, there was the case of Harry Price of Long Eaton, England. Given only a few weeks to live when he received a disability discharge from the army back in 1917, in 1969 he celebrated his 101st birthday!

That brings us around to the Carpenter's Way of life. People counted it out soon after it began. Down through the years it has continued to live and grow despite the fact that it was "supposed" to die. Just a few years back one of the famous Beatles singing group repeated this tale that "Christianity is on the way out."

For 2000 years men have been dooming His Way to death, but it continues to live. "On this rock I will build my church, and the powers of death shall not prevail against it." You know, I'm inclined to believe that He told the truth.

A Stone On:

"I'M IN SAD SHAPE"

Matthew 5:14a—*"You are the light of the world."*

Isn't it strange how the Father uses different media to speak to us. His most perfect revelation, of course, was His Son. And He speaks to us still through His Written Word. But this is not the only method He uses. He used other means such as a good book, a sermon, or a friend. He even uses the funny papers occasionally! He spoke to me recently through Peanuts.

In that Peanuts column Lucy was shown at her wayside stand with a sign reading: "Psychiatric Help—5¢. The doctor is in." Charlie Brown comes along and says, "I'm in sad shape. What can you do when you don't fit in? What can you do when life seems to be passing you by?" To this Lucy replies: "Follow me. I want to show you something. See the horizon over there? See how big it is? See how much room there is for everybody? Have you ever seen any other world?" "No," says Charlie Brown. "As far as you know this is the only world there is—right?" "Right!" replies Charlie Brown.

Lucy shouts: "Well, live in it then!" Whereupon Charlie Brown does one of his famous somersaults.

Many of us are like Charlie Brown. We think we are in sad shape. We mope along with our fears and worries. We go in for self-pity. We look here and there for help—without finding it. We think the world has given us a raw deal. We go around hunting only for the bad. We are in bad shape ourselves. We get to thinking that the faith of the Nazarene is dull and ordinary. Too many who bear His name are down-at-the-mouth.

Then along comes the Divine Psychiatrist. He takes us by the hand and shows us the wide and wonderful world in which we live, this mystery and wonder of life, this sparkling bit of time and space that is all ours for a brief moment of history. He tells us that we are the salt of the earth, the light of the world. He tells us that there is a Father Who knows us better than we know ourselves, a Maker that is closer than the air we breathe. He says that our Father loves us beyond our comprehension, even more than an earthly father loves his son.

But He does more than this. He shames us for our timidity, and our crankiness. He dissolves our guilt and restores our faith in God and ourselves. He Himself is our key to abundant living. He shouts to us across the centuries to live in our world as though we were citizens of the eternities. It is He and He alone Who puts meaning into our existence and purpose into our lives. He gives the ring of divine ordination to the most trivial of all occupations.

Through His speaking we hear Him saying that He came that we could find life, abundant life. Great is the number seeking for that abundant life. It is a pity that they think it can be found in rings and things.

If we are in sad shape, we might not need to turn Charlie Brown's somersault, but we might need to take another look at our world—and our God and ourself. Who knows, we might just want to turn that somersault with old Charlie after taking that look!

A Stone On:
A VISIT TO THE DENTIST

John 3:3—*"Jesus answered him, 'Truly, truly, I say to you, unless one is born anew he cannot see the kingdom of God."*

I did something recently which I didn't want to do, but should have done some time ago. All of us have a nature to put off something which we should do, delay it, wait until the very last moment to get it done. For me it was a visit to the dentist to have a tooth filled.

I should have gone some time ago. Fact about the business is that my tooth had had a cavity for several years and it was continually getting worse. And, over a period of years, I had consistently put off doing something I should have done long ago. But finally I gathered enough nerve, and time, to get the dentist to check it out.

I went to the dentist expecting full well that the tooth would be pulled, that I had waited too long to have any hopes—and certainly any right— to expect the dentist to save my tooth. But the dentist checked it out, found the roots in good

28

condition and the nerves alive, and proceeded to fill that tooth and save it!

I must confess that it was somewhat painful to have the tooth renewed. The nerves were very much alive, and several times I felt the grind of the drill on the nerve. Several times I tensed my muscles while the dentist was removing the decay.

After that visit, it suddenly dawned on me that I had experienced a great theological truth. And one of the finest sermons ever preached to me had been preached by the dentist. But he never knew it. Shall I share that theological truth with you?

I put off doing what I should have done long ago. This is human nature. How many of us should have made a visit to our Maker's presence long ago, only to put it off. When I finally did go, it was out of a sense of desperation. And isn't this, too, human nature. We put off any dealings with our Father till our life is about spent and we feel the situation is desperate.

And when I did go I felt the tooth was too far gone. I had no hopes of saving it. Again, many who come to the Father consider their lives too rotten, too far gone to cleanse and save. It hurt getting all the old decayed portion removed. This, too, is the way it is with life. It hurts to admit all our sins, to see ourselves as we really are. It hurts to confess our mistakes, to say we were wrong. The pain of the drill was necessary. So is the pain of confession.

Perhaps the most important part is that I came away with a new tooth. And after the pain and hurt is over, our Father gives us a new lease on life. We can come away with the decay of sin gone, and a clean life in front of us.

I guess many of us are with the Father like I was with the dentist—we have put it off too long already. If you are reading this, and there is still life in your roots, there is still hope. Better not wait any longer to make that visit.

Of course, if you are reading this and feel no pain for wrongdoing, it could be that the roots of the soul are already dead.

A Stone On:
WE HAVE CHEATED OUR CHILDREN

Proverbs 22:6a—*"Train up a child in the way he should go . . ."*

We have cheated our children! They have the best chance at a good education, and countless opportunities belong to them in the business world. They have never had a time in history when their chance of making a good living was as good as it is now. But they are cheated! Robbed! And it is the parents who are to blame.

Over in Vietnam a young soldier named Terry J. lay wounded and near death. He was caught in a battle and saw no way to escape alive. So, following what he considered to be his final living minutes, he wrote a letter to his mother. The Bristol, Virginia, Herald Courier carried the letter later. Here is the updated version of what he said.

"Dear Mother: You let us down! You never taught us to pray . . . and you never even sent us to Sunday School where somebody else could have done so. Yet there I was, right on the brink of eternity, and I didn't even know how to commence

31

or what to say to the Lord. So please correct this error before Bud and Sis get away from home! Luckily for me, our chaplain has befriended me. But it is an awful sensation to face death and not even know how to speak to God."

I didn't make it up. I just clipped it from the paper. And the story is true. It happened just that way. So you see, our children are cheated! And we parents are the ones to blame. Shame on us for giving our children everything in life except that which they shall eternally need! Shame on those of us who call ourselves parents and yet raise our families ignorant of life's greatest riches! Twice shame upon us! We are guilty and the error is on our record.

Another soldier wrote the following poem. It, too, speaks of the way our children are cheated.

"Look God, I have never spoken to you,
    but now—
I want to say: "How do you do?" You see
    God, they
Told me you didn't exist.
And like a fool—I believed all of this.
Last night from a shell-hole I saw your sky—
I figured right then they had told me a lie.
Had I taken the time to see the things you made,
I'd know they weren't calling a spade a spade.
I wonder, God, if you'd shake my hand,
Somehow—I feel that you will understand.
Funny, I had to come to this hellish place,
Before I had time to see your face.

Well, I guess there isn't much more to say
But I'm sure glad, God, I met you today.
I guess the zero-hour will soon be here
But I'm not afraid since I know you are here.
The signal—well, God—I'll have to go,
I like you lots—this I want you to know.
Looks like this will be a horrible fight.
Who knows—I may come to your house tonight.
Though I wasn't friendly with you before,
I wonder, God—if you'd wait at the door—
Look—I am crying, me shedding tears,
I wish I'd known you these many years.
Well, I'll have to go now, God—goodbye.
Strange—since I met you—I'm not afraid to die.

The poem isn't made up. It was found on a 19-year-old soldier in Vietnam. The sad part is that he was dead.

Our children are cheated.

A Stone On:
THE EASTER STORY IS TRUE

Mark 16:6—"*And he said to them, 'Do not be amazed; you seek Jesus of Nazareth, who was crucified. He has risen, he is not here; see the place where they laid him.'*"

A lot of people will call me stupid, I know. Some will feel sorry for me. Others will snicker a little and say that I should grow up. We humans have a way of expressing our feelings without ever uttering a word. And reading all the expressions I may come to the conclusion that this will be the attitude of many toward me.

But it doesn't really matter what others think of me. What is important is what I think of myself and what the Carpenter thinks of me. Somehow, if I have His approval and blessing all the other snide remarks seem to have a way of diminishing in importance. So I guess that's the reason that what others think just isn't too important. Their opinion being relatively unimportant, I feel free to make the following known about myself.

I believe it happened. I believe that, basically, it happened just the way we have been taught it happened. I believe they took a just Man—the most just Man ever to walk on the face of this earth—and they nailed Him to a tree. I believe they did it because of their selfishness and sinfulness. I believe He allowed it to happen. I believe that He had the power to stop it, destroy them all if He wished. But I believe He allowed them to do it because of His great love. I believe it broke His heart, that inside He wanted so much to be loved by those who sought to destroy Him.

I believe that He forgave them, that He held no bitterness nor hatred toward them. And I believe that, in the irony of it all, His love was stronger than their hate. I believe that to this very day the most powerful weapon in the universe is the power of the love of the Galilean Carpenter. I believe there is no weapon anywhere that can make a dent in it. And I believe that the only cure, yes I said the only cure, to the basic troubles of the world today is the application of that love in our lives. I am convinced that it has always been and will continue to be His will for us to love one another like He loves us.

Yes, I believe that He did arise from the grave. I believe that He was fully dead when removed from the cross and placed in the tomb. And I am convinced beyond a shadow of a doubt that He conquered death with life, that He came alive again and lives today and will live forever. Add to that my belief that it is His greatest wish for us that we live that life with Him here and now and in the life that is beyond death.

No, I cannot explain it. No one can. But I can experience it. Everyone can. No, I'm not perfect. I am a miserable creature, unworthy of anything on my own merits. But I have a Saviour, and therefore I no longer need to depend on my own merits —only my faith.

Laugh. Snicker. Call me stupid. I guess that is the highest compliment you could pay me. But don't do it too loud. It could be that one day you might share my beliefs.

A Stone On:
FINDING LIFE BEAUTIFUL

John 10:10b—*"I came that they may have life, and have it abundantly."*

In the year 1931, Aldous Huxley, the famous skeptic, wrote on the subject: "Wanted, a New Pleasure." In the essay, he said: "As far as I can see the only possible new pleasure would be derived from the invention of a new drug which would provide a harmless substitute for alcohol. If I were a millionaire, I should endow a band of research workers to look for the ideal intoxicant. If we could sniff or swallow something that would abolish inferiority, atone us with our fellows in a glowing exultation of affection and make life in all its aspects seem not only worth living but divinely beautiful and significant, and if this heavenly world-transforming drug were of such a kind that we could wake up next morning with a clear head and undamaged constitution, then it seems to me that all our problems would be solved and earth would be a paradise."

Huxley was hunting something we all hunt in

life. Every person seeks what he wanted. The difference comes in the methods in which we seek it. For him, and countless others, the answer could be found in a drug or a bottle. Some kind of magic to turn the trick.

Some of the rest of us have found that which Huxley searched for, but we didn't find it in the magic of a bottle. We found it in the miracle of a Cross. We have followed the little Jew tentmaker's advice: "Do not get drunk with wine, which will only ruin you; instead, be filled with the Spirit." Abolish inferiority? We have rid ourselves of it by hearing Him tell us that we are "the light of the world . . . the salt of the earth." And when He compares us with terms like those we cannot feel inferior.

Affection toward our fellows? We have found that, too. You see, the Galilean has taught us to do exactly what Mr. Huxley wanted—to love one another. He set the example. He loved us. "Greater love has no man than this . . ." Then, because of His love, He faced that Cross.

And something to make life more than mere existing? Some, who follow the Galilean, can say with Him: ". . . for this purpose I have come . . ." And making life beautiful? There is nothing more beautiful in all of life than to see it as His creation. To know that He is there, behind it all, full of love for us even when we don't deserve it, makes life eternally beautiful. He is, indeed, the Source of all beauty!

A clear head and undamaged constitution? He gives that, too. Let's you think clearly and live with a constitution written by the Author of Life.

Mr. Huxley kept hunting for that "magic" drug. On November 22, 1963, thirty-one years after his wish, Huxley tried a new drug called LSD which many thought to be the answer to his wish. His wife administered the drug to Huxley, dying of cancer. It was the last drug Huxley ever experimented with. You see, it was a one-way trip.

A Stone On:

THE GREAT DREAM

Genesis 37:19—"*They said to one another, 'Here comes this dreamer.'*"

We used to be a nation of dreamers. Some of that is missing now, but we have it as part of our heritage. Our forefathers, those who founded our country were dreamers. They dreamed of a country where man would be free, where he could live in dignity and hope and promise of a better tomorrow.

They lived that dream, believed in it so much they were willing to give their lives for it. Nothing could stop them from reaching out for that dream— not even all the combined power of the King of England. They took that dream and with it they beat the unbeatable foe, they conquered the unconquerable land, they traveled the untravelable roads. What great dreamers they were!

But they were not the greatest dreamers this world has had. There was a small group of men who had even greater dreams than did the founders of our country. Back nearly two thousand years ago there was a group of eleven men who had a dream—a great dream. They dreamed that they could conquer the world without ever lifting a sword or firing a gun. They dreamed that one day every man, woman, and child could and would share with them the new faith they had found. They dreamed that one day this world would be ruled by love.

It was a great dream they had—so great, in fact, that the world laughed at them, ridiculed them, even persecuted and killed them. But the dream could not be destroyed. It lived on. They planted that dream of a world ruled by love in the hearts and minds of other men. The dream lived and grew. Soon that dream had conquered men of all climates, all classes, all races.

There are those who are still dreaming that dream today. They are inspired by a Carpenter Who touched the hearts of common men as no other Man. He planted that dream in their hearts, nourished it, watched it grow. It is the dream of a world where men are brothers, where we help instead of hurt, share instead of steal, give instead of grab. It is a dream of a world ruled by brotherly love.

A foolish dream? An unrealistic dream? An illogical dream? Yes, it has been called all those things. But that doesn't stop men from dreaming it and from trying to make that dream come true. It is, in a way, an unfulfilled dream. But, men still search after it.

The call goes out from this Galilean Carpenter

today for more dreamers. Few there are who dare to give themselves to that dream. It seems unreachable to most people. It is certainly a big dream, and requires the best there is in a man. For this reason, very few dare dream that dream. For it is a challenge, the world's greatest challenge. It isn't a dream for sissies, or weaklings, or lazy men. No, it is a dream for men, great men.

If you are a dreamer looking for a dream to give yourself to, there is none greater in all the world. And one day, with His help, the dream will come true.

A Stone On:
EARNING OUR RESPECT

Romans 13:7—*"Pay all of them their dues, taxes to whom taxes are due, revenue to who revenue is due, respect to whom respect is due, honor to whom honor is due."*

The little five-year-old boy came home after playing with several of his friends. Speaking of one of his little playmates, he told his father that his small friend had used a bad word. "What did he say, son?" asked his father. The little boy replied: "He said nigger."

You see, the small boy had been taught to say "negro" and not "nigger." He had been taught that he should respect his fellow man. Many times he had been corrected when he mispronounced the word. He had come to know that there was a proper way of pronouncing the word and a slurring method.

Couldn't we all use a little more of what the little boy had? Respect, I mean. Wouldn't it be a better world if the white man would treat the colored man with more respect? And wouldn't our relationship be so much better if the colored man would treat the white man with that same respect?

It doesn't cost anything to be nice, and it solves so many problems. There is so much hatred, and ugliness, and disrespect in our world that there just isn't room for any more. And certainly we don't need any more. We don't trust each other, we try to cheat each other, we show contempt for each other. It has become so very expensive to go this route. Saying "negro" doesn't require any extra effort, just a little respect. And "whitey" coming from the lips of a colored person doesn't make them any bigger or better.

Respect means we have to be respectable. All of us could learn from that. Instead of trying to place the blame on another race, we could begin by making ourselves a little more respectable. I'm speaking about all of us, all races. If we want another race to respect us it means that we are going to have to be respectable. It means that we must make ourselves so worthy of respect that people cannot keep from respecting us.

Where there is hatred, we must replace it with love. Where there is prejudice, we must replace it with justice. Where there is disrespect, we must replace it with respectability. Now accomplishing this is no easy job. But He can help us do it. And we will never be able to accomplish it without His help. Burning cities isn't going to make our country any better, neither is relegating any group of people to a second-class role. But He can make our country better, if we will allow Him to make us better. It is certain that our country will never be any better unless we are.

The story about the five-year-old is true. The boy's father was real proud of the boy, too. I know. You see, he's my son.

A Stone On:
WILL WE LEARN BEFORE IT'S TOO LATE?

I Corinthians 13:4–5—*"Love is patient and kind; love is not jealous or boastful; it is not arrogant or rude. Love does not insist on it's own way; it is not irritable or resentful."*

Couldn't we learn to love each other? Before it is too late, before we go too far, before we destroy the earth and everything there is on it, couldn't we learn to love each other? Don't turn me off, don't call me a fanatic, don't say I'm off my rocker. For the chances are growing greater and greater every day that we will destroy each other unless we learn to love each other.

We have missiles strung around the world, missiles that have but one purpose—to kill. We humans annually spend more money on weapons than on any other single item. Some people call it progress, this ability to kill more than your enemy. The Galilean says it is suicide.

"Love your enemy . . ." No, we can't do that, can we? "It won't work," we say. How do we know it won't work, we haven't tried it. We have been too busy inventing more deadly weapons. It could very well be that the most powerful weapon in all the world is to practice the Galilean's Way, to "love your enemy." We have worked on the assumption that the only way to get rid of our enemy is to destroy him, kill him. But don't you get rid of your enemy when you make him your friend?

Couldn't we learn to love each other? Before somebody accidently pushes the wrong button at the right time, couldn't we learn to be brothers? Do we have to destroy this earth, blow it to pieces, because of our sinfulness? Couldn't we find a way to work things out?

We have declared war on poverty in this country. We have set out to improve everybody's lot. We are going to try to give everybody a fair share. That's ok. But we are only by-passing the real war on poverty. Our greatest poverty is in the spiritual realm. The very area that made us great we have now placed last. We are poor. We have more than we have ever had before, we eat better than we have ever eaten, and we spend more now than ever before in history. But we are poor. Starving. Dying. We have nothing to undergird us, to tie us together, to help us understand ourselves and get along with our fellowman. Couldn't we learn to love each other?

We take liquor and bottle it and sell it and tax it and drink it by the millions of gallons. We take tobacco and roll it and sell it and tax it and smoke it by the tons. We take sex, pervert it, film it, print

47

it, and market it voluminously and call it freedom. We hate each other because of the color of our skin, or the size of our income, or because someone can do something a little better than we can. And all these things are only symptoms of a sickness, a sickness in the soul of man. It is hungering for something we are denying it. It is crying out for it's Creator.

What a grand place to live we could have if we could only learn to love one another as He loves us. Couldn't we learn to do that? Couldn't we? Before it is too late?

A Stone On:

PURPOSE

John 12:27b—*"No, for this purpose I have come to this hour."*

I met an old friend the other day. When he asked me to have coffee with him, I took him up on the offer. I'm glad I did. For my visit with him did much to restore my faith in mankind.

During the conversation with him, it happened to turn toward two friends of ours that we knew from our high school days. My friend told me about the two, how good the jobs they had, how much money they were making, and the way they lived. "They have got their own business now," he said, "and evidently are making a killing. But you know what? They haven't changed a bit. They are the same as always. Life to them is one big party after another. They make big money, dress sharp to impress their business associates, drive expensive automobiles, and drink their high-priced booze while chasing their women."

My friend went on to tell me that one of the two had recently gotten a divorce. "He's dating plenty of sharp chicks now," he said. "They live in fast company." Then my friend kinda shocked me by what he said. "That's a heck of a way to live," he said. "To know you have got to do that day after day. To go to bed drunk and get up with a hangover and then to know that you have to go through it again that night would be a heck of a way to live."

You know, I got to thinking about that. Here was a friend of mine, a traveling salesman, who gets his kicks from making a good home for a wife and son, saying that if there was no purpose any higher in life than living it up and having a ball, then he would find it extremely difficult to find life worth living. For him there had to be some purpose behind it all.

Isn't this precisely the feeling that we are created with? To have some goal in life, some purpose, something to work toward? Here is another Man, walking along the shores of the Sea of Galilee, teaching, preaching, healing, saying that "for this purpose I have come." The purpose gave so much meaning to His life that He gave His life for that purpose.

In a classroom behind the Iron Curtain some years ago the professor was without an answer for a question posed by one of the pupils. "Prof," the pupil asked, "what's the purpose of life?" A Galilean had an answer to the question. He said the purpose of life is to serve, both God and fellowman.

Maybe we should, instead of complaining about

all our concerns, rejoice that we have something to be concerned about. For no one is to be pitied more in life than the person whose major goal is to make more money and whose greatest joy comes from carelessness.

"Thank you, Lord, for values greater than money and goals higher than pleasure."

A Stone On:
THE GREEN GATE HAS CLOSED

Psalms 34:8—"O taste and see that the Lord is good! Happy is the man who takes refuge in him."

For 17 years the Green Gate was a striptease club in San Antonio, Texas. All kinds of people came to the Green Gate. Some were lonely people seeking companionship. Some were frustrated people, trying to sap a temporary thrill from a life that had no meaning. Some were ignorant people who thought life offered nothing higher than a bottle of booze and a naked dame.

The Green Gate is closed now. It's out of business. It wasn't so much a lack of business that closed the Green Gate. It was more of a change of attitude on the part of the owner. Guy Linton closed down his club and said it will stay closed. Linton even posted a sign over the club door which read: "Closed Forever."

There's many clubs like the Green Gate still in operation across the country. Thousands of them. There people can go to find lights low, music loud, and booze plentiful. Many of them do a thriving business, living off the superficial food they offer to the deep hunger in the human heart.

Dr. Gallup ran a poll on happiness many years ago. He found that the most unhappy people were those who visited the taverns and clubs. *Life* magazine said some time back that we spend more than forty billion dollars a year seeking this elusive thing known as happiness.

Will Rogers, a man of a day gone by, used to tell about a druggist who was asked if he ever took time off from his duties to have a good time. The druggist said that he did not, but that he sold a lot of headache medicine to those who did.

What is a good time? How do you define it? Is it something that has no lasting value in it, is gone when you wake up the next morning? Or is it the deep satisfaction that comes from knowing you are drinking deep from the cup of life offered by the Father? Surely happiness comes from having some great objective, beneficial to mankind, and single-mindedly pursuing that objective with all the strength in oneself.

Some of those who are seeking happiness in the clubs and taverns are surprised when they finally find happiness. They are surprised to find that it comes not from a club but from a Cause. A great and demanding Cause. Guy Linton found it in this manner. You see, Linton made his decision to close the Green Gate after listening to Rev. Bob Harrington, the "Chaplain of Bourbon Street," speak to a standing-room-only crowd. Now Guy

Linton has, to use familiar words, "changed over to the Lord's side."

But don't worry about the Green Gate. Linton has said that the Green Gate will be turned into a religious bookstore. Let's hope the Green Gate keeps its same customers that it has had for many years.

And unless other club owners are ready to close down their clubs, we advise them to stay away from the Man of Galilee.

A Stone On:
A LOT ON A LITTLE

Luke 6:48a—*"He is like a man building a house, who dug deep, and laid the foundation upon rock."*

Have you ever watched one of those long freight trains go past? Some of them seem like they are a mile long, don't they? I once counted a hundred fourteen boxcars on one of those long ones. Sometimes you wonder how those tracks can hold such a heavy load. Well, it is hard to believe but a train of one hundred cars and weighing 26,000,-000 pounds is supported at any given moment on an area totaling only a little more than two square feet! (2.06 square feet is the exact number.) That is hard to believe, isn't it? Yet it is true. A hundred-car train that weighs 26,000,000 pounds is supported by just more than two square feet! The reason that such a tremendous load is supported by such a small territory is that the railroad has a good foundation.

Whether or not the folks who built the railroad were Christian or not we cannot say. But one thing is for certain, they used one principle taught by the Galilean in their building of the railroad. They laid a good foundation.

Now the Carpenter was talking about a different type of foundation than that laid for a railroad track. He was talking about a foundation for your belief in God and trust in His will. Jesus said the best way to build a foundation was to be active doing those things that He said do. He likened those who heard his words and acted upon them to the man who built his house on the rock. He likened those who only heard His word and did not act accordingly to the man who built his house on the sand. Even if you have never heard this teaching of Christ, you know the result of each man's building.

When your trust in God is built by a firm faith in God and a strong desire to do His will, you will be able to stand the storms of life that inevitably face each one of us. Death is one of those storms. Tragedy is another. Pain could be added to the list. Jesus said these will not shake your faith if it is rooted not only in the hearing but also the doing of His words.

Any builder will tell you that the foundation is one of the most important parts of building. If the foundation isn't strong, the rest of the building is in danger and probably will suffer damage if put to a test. Just recently the newspapers carried the picture of an apartment building in New Orleans where the builders had to drive several stabilizers over one hundred fifty feet into the ground to insure a solid foundation for the multistory apartment building. Now Jesus taught that we should have a solid foundation for our lives also.

Partly, and maybe mostly, what is wrong with the world today, and especially our country, is that we don't have a solid foundation underneath us to sustain us. Too many times we want a prefabricated Christian experience that comes in a neat little package and doesn't interfere with our lives in any manner. This type of foundation suits us just fine till the storm hits and then we wish we had a more solid foundation because we see our building crumbling on the weak foundation that we have built.

Now it was probably a great surprise to you that the one hundred-car train was supported on less than three square feet. For those of you who are outside the Christian faith it will come as a surprise also to learn that the Christian has built his foundation on nothing but the Galilean. That seems an awfully small foundation, doesn't it? Just one man. But the record speaks for itself: He is sufficient.

A Stone On:

A DROP AT A TIME

Psalms 90:12—*"So teach us to number our days that we may get a heart of wisdom."*

A faucet in your home that drips once a second could waste over seven hundred gallons of water in one year's time! It doesn't seem possible that one little drip could be so destructive but it is. We are fooled because of it's smallness and we underestimate it's potential.

The same thing happens with our money. We spend a dollar here and a quarter there and before you know it our pay check is gone. We don't really think we are spending a lot when we spend a dollar or a quarter, but it won't be long before we begin to see that dollars and quarters add up.

Now let us move into the area of daily life. We humans waste a lot of our life. We piddle around day by day, thinking we have plenty of time, and then one day we suddenly realize that our life is almost gone! Because we only live a day at a time it is sometimes hard for us to tie our days together to see that they make weeks and months and years. The Psalmist had this in mind when he wrote, "So teach us to number our days . . ."

Lots of us need to start numbering our days. For instance, what did you do yesterday that was worthwhile for someone else? Or what are you going to do today that will help make this world a better place to live in? Most of us have some big plans that we really mean to fulfill, except we let the days slip away and never get around to fulfilling our plans. We don't really mean to waste time, it just is gone before we know it. And each minute that slips away is gone from our reach forever. It can never be recalled for us.

Paul had this in mind when he wrote, "Be urgent in season and out of season." Robert Herrick also had the thought in mind when he wrote the little poem we like to say:

> "Gather ye rosebuds while ye may,
> Old Time is still a-flying,
> And this same flower that smiles today,
> Tomorrow will be dying."

My friends, this life that we live is so short that we should work each day with a purpose in our lives. We shouldn't merely exist from day to day and take whatever blind fate turns our way. We should plan and work, and work and plan. And we ought to do it all in the firm faith that the Carpenter is the Author of Life. Peter had a reason in mind when he used this term to speak of Him. When an author begins to write a book, he has a plan in mind by which to proceed. Peter was saying that the Creator has a plan for your life because He is the Author of Life. You and I will never find any real purpose in life apart from the Author of Life. This is the reason we need to tune our lives to God's purpose.

You come back to it again and again. That is, that the only thing lasting in this old world is God's work. That is what we should do. We should work for God. Remember how He once said, "How is it that ye sought me? wist ye not I must be about my Father's Business?" We need to get busy about our Father's business. And I'm not talking about Daddy's furniture store, or farm, or station, either. Now don't misunderstand. You can certainly do the Father's business in the furniture store, or on the farm, or at the station. And you should do His business there. That's all I'm saying. Work for Him wherever you are. You will be richer because of it. And others will be, also. And the world will be a better place because you were a part of it.

A Stone On:
SEEKING HAPPINESS IN THE LITTLE PILL

Matthew 6:33—"*But seek first his kingdom and his righteousness, and all these things shall be yours as well.*"

It is a funny age in which you and I are living. We have more now than any people in the history of mankind. We earn the highest wages, eat more of the best food, wear more of the finest clothes, live better in well constructed houses, travel farther by faster and more comfortable means, retire earlier and live longer. All this, and we are, in some respects, the most miserable people ever!

The American Chemical Society estimates that normal Americans use thirty-two million dollars worth of tranquilizers. Another twenty-five million dollars worth is given to patients in mental hospitals. And now listen to this: about one out of twelve Americans take tranquilizers regularly. But take heart, tranquilizer takers! There are some thirty varieties to choose from. You can have your choice!

Dr. Herbert Ratner says that America is the most overmedicated, overoperated, overinoculated,

61

and yet the most anxiety-ridden country in all the world. We suffer most from so-called diseases of civilization, including neuroses, high blood pressure, ulcers (anybody have one?) and heart disease. And here is a figure that is appalling to any sensible man—suicide is the fourth cause of all deaths between the ages of fifteen and forty-four. In the years in which life is supposed to be the greatest, suicide ranks fourth in the taking of lives!

The trouble is, according to Dr. Ratner, we look upon mental and physical health as a commodity to be bought in the supermarket. "We have been increasingly a paying animal, whereas we have become decreasingly a praying animal, as if spiritual repose were unrelated to total health," says Dr. Ratner.

The secret here, you see, is that being sound physically and mentally doesn't complete the man. It will any other animal but not man. Man has about him a spiritual side which is ever more important than the physical or mental. Whether we are willing to admit it or not, mind and body and spirit affect each other—for good or ill.

The Man of Galilee had a word to say here. "Seek first his kingdom," He said, "and his righteousness, and all these things . . ." He knew only too well that happiness comes from wholeness. This may well be one interpretation of the Beatitudes. "Blessed are they," He said. And here He is saying that the happy people are those who relate themselves to themselves, to others, to their world, and to the Creator in the way He intended for them to do when He made them.

It is a funny thing indeed that those who are seeking desperately for happiness never find it, and those who are too busy doing something worthwhile to seek happiness are the most happy.

It is true, then, that the deep wisdom of the Carpenter of Nazareth taught man nearly two thousand years ago still rings true today. Many who have failed to find comfort in tranquilizers have come to find the truth in that statement. Give this statement a try in your life today: "Seek first his kingdom and his righteousness, and all these things shall be yours as well."

You will be mighty glad you did!